Clarinet

Level 2–3

Selections from

A STEVEN SPIELBERG FILM

INDIANA JONES

and the
KINGDOM OF
THE CRYSTAL SKULL ™

PARAMOUNT PICTURES PRESENTS A LUCASFILM LTD. PRODUCTION A STEVEN SPIELBERG FILM HARRISON FORD "INDIANA JONES AND THE KINGDOM OF THE CRYSTAL SKULL" CATE BLANCHETT KAREN ALLEN RAY WINSTONE JIM BROADBENT AND SHIA LABEOUF CASTING BY DEBRA ZANE C.S.A. VISUAL EFFECTS & ANIMATION BY INDUSTRIAL LIGHT & MAGIC MUSIC BY JOHN WILLIAMS EDITED BY MICHAEL KAHN A.C.E. COSTUME DESIGNED BY MARY ZOPHRES CO-PRODUCER DENIS L. STEWART DIRECTOR OF PHOTOGRAPHY JANUSZ KAMINSKI EXECUTIVE PRODUCERS GEORGE LUCAS KATHLEEN KENNEDY PRODUCED BY FRANK MARSHALL STORY BY GEORGE LUCAS AND JEFF NATHANSON SCREENPLAY BY DAVID KOEPP DIRECTED BY STEVEN SPIELBERG

IndianaJones.com

Alfred Publishing Co., Inc.
16320 Roscoe Blvd., Suite 100
P.O. Box 10003
Van Nuys, CA 91410-0003
alfred.com

Arranged by Bill Galliford, Ethan Neuburg and Tod Edmondson

ISBN-10: 0-7390-5661-1
ISBN-13: 978-0-7390-5661-5

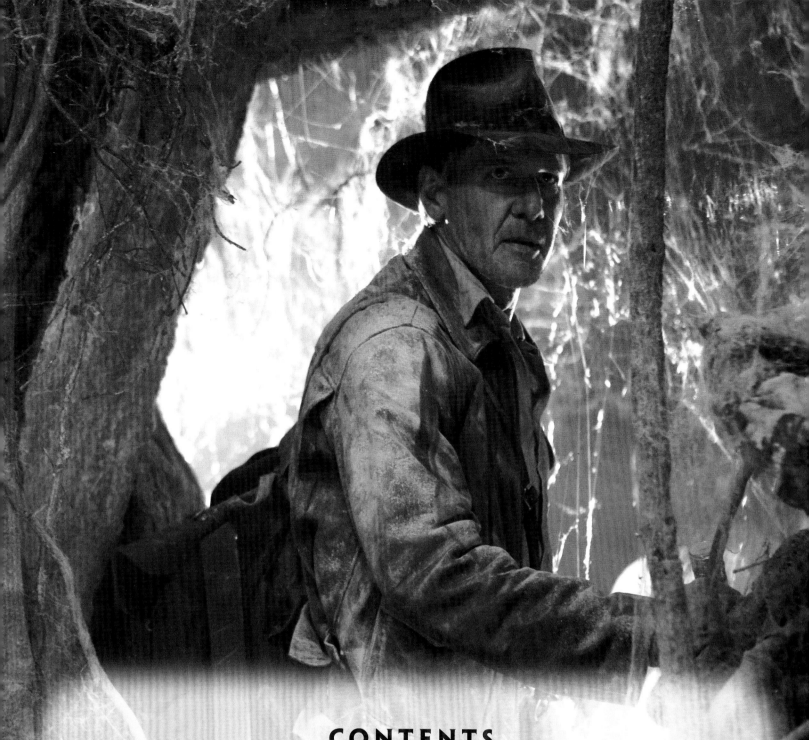

CONTENTS

	BOOK PAGE NUMBER	CD TRACK DEMO	PLAY-ALONG

MARION'S THEME
(as featured in RAIDERS MARCH)

Music by
JOHN WILLIAMS

Moderately slow, flowing (♩ = 104)

31761

RAIDERS MARCH

Music by
JOHN WILLIAMS

THE ADVENTURES OF MUTT

Music by
JOHN WILLIAMS

The Adventures of Mutt - 2 - 1
31761

9

IRINA'S THEME

Music by
JOHN WILLIAMS

THE JOURNEY TO AKATOR

Music by
JOHN WILLIAMS

With exuberance (♩. = 126)

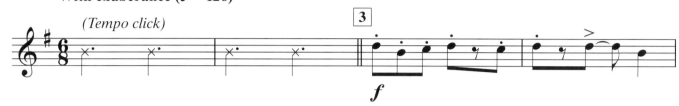

The Journey to Akator - 2 - 1
31761

PARTS OF A CLARINET AND FINGERING CHART

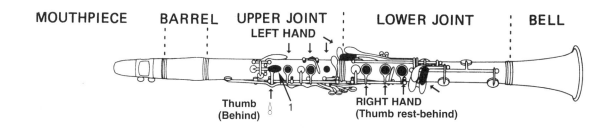

● = press the key or cover the hole with your finger.
○ = do not press the key or cover the hole.

When there is more than one fingering given for a note, use the first one unless the alternate fingering is suggested.

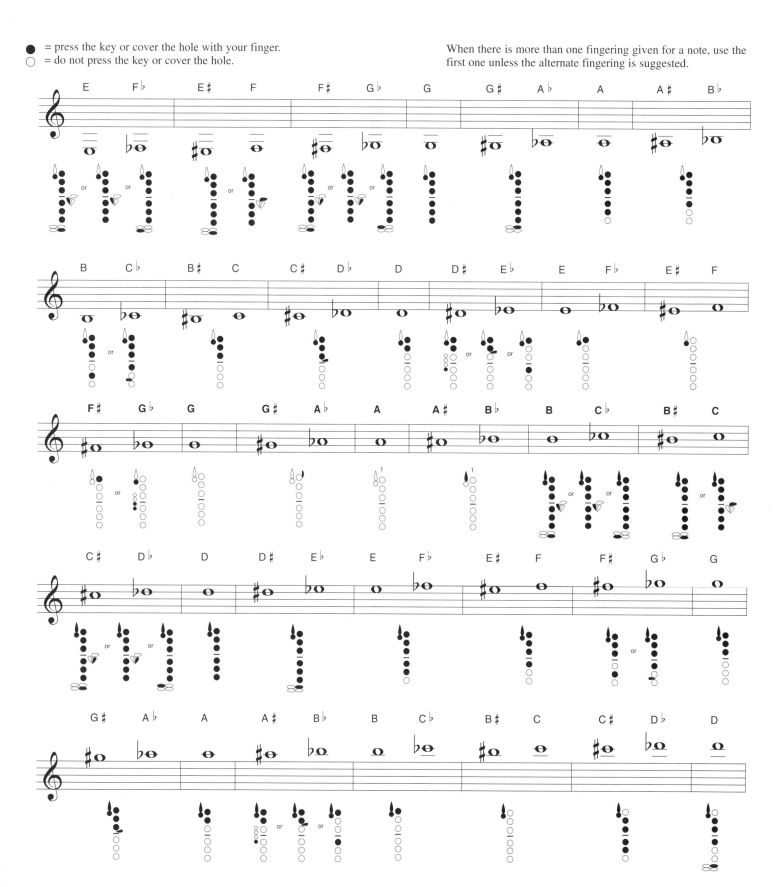